THROUGH THE EYES OF SEVENTEEN

IN THE SPACE BETWEEN DREAMS AND REALITY

SARGAM SINGH

Made with ❤ on the Notion Press Platform
www.notionpress.com

This book is dedicated to those who dare to feel deeply, who wrestle with their own truths and search for meaning in a world that often feels too loud. To the ones who stand in the silence, waiting for clarity amidst the chaos, and to those who have loved with a heart wide open, only to be broken and rebuilt. It is for the dreamers, the seekers, the lost souls, and the quiet warriors—those who navigate the storm and find strength in their vulnerability.

To anyone who has ever wondered who they are beneath the weight of others' expectations, or questioned their place in a world that seems to demand conformity, this is for you. May you find in these pages the courage to be unapologetically, impossibly, and beautifully yourself.

To the moon, the stars, and the vastness of the night sky, for reminding us that even in darkness, there is light. To the silence that teaches us more than words ever could, and to the love that carries us through the fiercest storms.

And finally, to the future selves we are becoming—may we always remember the strength we discovered in the quiet, the beauty we found in the brokenness, and the power we hold to rise, again and again.

Contents

Foreword

In the vast expanse of life, we are often cast into roles—by others, by society, and sometimes by ourselves. We wear labels that may not fit, carry weights that don't belong to us, and follow paths that never quite feel like our own. But what happens when the voice within begins to rise, when the urge to break free from the constraints of expectation calls louder than anything else? This book is the cry of that voice—a testament to the rebellion against the labels, the masks, and the stories that have tried to define us.

At seventeen, life is a contradiction. We are both the beginning and the end, the uncharted land and the map trying to make sense of it. We are learning, unlearning, growing, and breaking all at once. But more than anything, we are searching—for who we are, for what we want, and for the courage to embrace our true selves. In these pages, you will find raw, unfiltered emotions, poems that explore the struggles of being both too much and not enough, of longing for freedom from expectations, and the painful yet beautiful journey of self-discovery.

This collection is not just for those who have walked a similar path, but for anyone who has ever felt the weight of the world pressing down on them, anyone who has been caught between the self they wish to be and the self they are told to be. It's for anyone who has ever wondered: Who am I beneath the labels?

Here, in the rhythm of each line, you will find a reminder—that your journey, your story, is yours to write. The struggle is real, but so is the triumph. There is beauty in breaking free, in allowing yourself to exist without apology, without restriction. You will learn that to be lost is to be on the cusp of something greater. You will discover that to rise is to finally accept the truth of who you are.

So, take this journey with me. Through the highs and the lows, through the questioning and the answers, through the shadows and the light. Together, we will uncover the strength to stand unshaken, the courage to be unapologetically ourselves. This is a book about you, about me, about all of us—finding our place in a world that demands conformity, but in the end, can only thrive when we embrace our uniqueness.

Welcome to the journey of self-discovery. Welcome to the uncharted space where you are free.

Preface

In the quiet corners of our minds, where thoughts swirl like winds in a storm, there exists a longing—a yearning to understand the self, to understand the world. We all search, though some do so with a louder heart, some in silence, some in the arms of others, and some alone in the darkness of their own thoughts. This collection of poems, crafted from the fragments of my heart and mind, reflects the journey of seeking, of being, and of becoming.

At seventeen, I stand at the edge of a vast, uncharted ocean of time, where every wave that crashes is a moment, and every whisper of wind carries a story. These pages are not merely ink and paper; they are echoes of the experiences that have shaped me, the fears that have whispered in my ear, the dreams that have danced before me in the quiet of the night. This book is not just about me, but about you, too—the readers who will find fragments of their own reflections within these words.

The moon, the stars, the tides—nature has always spoken to me in the language of poetry, and through these verses, I try to give voice to the silence, to the unsaid, to the spaces we often leave unexplored. Here, you will find love and heartbreak, growth and loss, the agony of self-doubt and the triumph of self-discovery. But most of all, you will find a space for your own stories—a place where your thoughts can echo back at you, where your own emotions can find refuge in the words on these pages.

This is not a book with neat answers or easy resolutions. It is, instead, a journey—a map of the heart, as uncertain and beautiful as the path we walk in our own lives. Every poem is a reflection, a window into the chaos, the peace, the joy, and the sorrow that make us human. It is an invitation to explore what it means to be alive, to feel, to hurt, and to grow.

So, as you turn these pages, I ask you to listen—not just to the words, but to the spaces between them, to the silence that surrounds them. Let the poems speak to you, in ways both gentle and fierce, and allow them to lead you into your own exploration of who you are, who you were, and who you have yet to become.

In the end, this book is not just my story. It is a part of yours too.

Prologue

The world does not stop. It is constantly moving—shifting, growing, and yet, in the midst of all this motion, there are moments when everything seems to hold its breath. At seventeen, I find myself standing in that pause, caught between who I am and who I am meant to become. I am both lost and found in the same breath, walking a path that seems uncertain, unsure of where it will lead, but compelled to take the next step anyway.

This book, these words, are my attempt to make sense of the world through poetry. It's an exploration of what it means to be on the cusp of adulthood—feeling the weight of the years ahead while holding tightly to the fragile pieces of youth that are slipping away with every passing day. These poems are reflections of love and loss, confusion and clarity, pain and healing. They are the stories of finding and losing myself in moments that feel too big, too heavy, too much to carry.

But there is something beautiful about that, isn't there? The weight of it all. The uncertainty. The fear of being wrong and the courage it takes to try anyway. The sun sets, and the moon rises. The waves crash, and the storm calms. Life is constantly in motion, yet we have these pauses—these moments when we can finally breathe, when we can step back and try to understand what it all means.

This book isn't about finding all the answers. It's about the questions that shape us, the ones we can't quite put into words. It's about the stillness that can only be found when everything else falls silent. It's about the journey—the uncertainty of the road and the clarity that sometimes only comes after the storm.

If these pages speak to you, know that they are not just mine. They are for you, too. For anyone who has stood at the edge of something, unsure of whether to jump or turn away. For anyone who has questioned who they are, what they're meant for, or how they fit into a world that constantly changes. These are the words of someone still figuring it out. Someone still learning how to stand tall, despite the winds that howl around them.

So here we are, at the beginning of something unknown. And maybe that's the most honest thing we can say—we don't know. But perhaps in the not knowing, there is freedom. There is grace. There is peace.

Welcome to this journey. Let it unfold, as we learn what it means to be fully alive.

1. Through the Eyes of Seventeen

At 17, the world's a scream,
a shattered glass, a splintered dream.
The hours blur, the moments flee,
"Does anyone truly see me for me?"

The sun is fire, the moon is frost,
I am found, yet I feel so damn lost.
A tempest trapped in fragile skin,
In a war I never wanted to win.
Who am I beneath the masks I've crafted?
Do I even exist, or am I just a shadow cast
by the expectations of others, even though they judge my past?
Their voices haunt me—my own smothered,
Lost in their words, suffocated, unheard.

Each breath I take feels like a fight,
to find the dawn in endless night.
I wear my scars like hidden art,
a tapestry stitched from a fractured heart.

They say, "Be brave, stand tall, hold on,"
but courage feels so far and gone.
I'm both the builder and the break,
a fragile soul that quakes and aches.

The stars above, they mock my name,
their icy glimmers dim my flame.
"Shine brighter, bolder, reach the sky!"
But what if I was meant to cry?

At 17, I'm fire and ash,
a fleeting spark, a lightning crash.
I write not just to heal the pain,
but feel alive in pouring rain.

My pen's a blade, my words, a prayer,
a soft rebellion against despair.
I write to carve through what's unspoken,
to fix the parts of me that's broken.

For who I am, I cannot say.
I'm lost, yet yearning, day by day.
And in the noise, I'll leave my mark,
a blazing star within the dark.

So read these words, and hear my cry,
a hymn for those who question why.
At 17, I'm fierce, I'm free,
and one day, you'll remember me.

SARGAM SINGH

Ripples of Reflection

17, the world feels too heavy. There's an emptiness in the spaces between the hours, a silence that echoes louder than any noise. I wear this weight like a second skin, suffocating beneath the expectations, the judgment, the endless pursuit of a version of myself that I can never quite reach. I look into the mirror and see someone I don't fully recognize—caught between who I was and who I'm expected to be. In the chaos of it all, I'm just trying to find a place where I can breathe, where I can be more than the sum of my fears. Every decision feels like a choice between living up to someone else's dream or breaking free, but I don't know how to do either without losing a part of myself. The world looks at me, and they see potential, but all I feel is the weight of unspoken words, of paths never chosen. I try to scream, but my voice is lost in the noise. So I write, hoping that one day someone might hear me, that in the quiet of my words, they'll understand what it feels like to be trapped in a world that's moving too fast, with too many expectations, and no map to guide the way. But you know, even in the darkest moments, there's a flicker—barely noticeable, yet enough to hold on to. It's the sliver of hope that whispers in the quietest corners, telling me that even when I don't know who I am, I am still someone with a mind and soul. The world may never stop pushing, and I may never fully find my place, but at least I can keep moving. One step forward, one word at a time. Maybe one day, I'll look back and realize that all these moments of doubt, pain, and confusion weren't wasted—they were the pieces that formed me. The shattered glass, the scattered dreams, they'll make sense in time. But for now, I'll keep writing, keep fighting, keep searching—for I am still here, still breathing, and that's something worth holding on to.

2. The mold

They told me I was clay—soft, unformed,
Perfect for shaping, for being adorned.
"Bend here, twist there, don't resist," they'd say,
"And you'll be perfect in every way."

So, I let their hands sculpt my skin,
Taught to obey, never to begin.
Each curve, each edge, they smoothed with care,
Until nothing of me was truly there.
I was praised for the beauty they'd made me to be,
Yet trapped in a form that wasn't truly me.
I felt their approval but not the air,
A masterpiece gasping, stripped and bare.

The mold fit snug, a gilded embrace,
Hiding the cracks they didn't erase.
They called me complete, a shining design,
But beneath it all, the flaws were mine.
Each time I tried to stretch or grow,
The mold resisted, it screamed, "No!"
"You'll break, you'll ruin the art we've built,
Stay still, or you'll drown in your guilt."

And I stayed, afraid, for years on end,

Shackled by fear, a mannequin to mend.
But deep inside, a spark remained,
A quiet fire I couldn't contain.
One day, the mold became too tight,
It cut through my soul; it dimmed my light.
In that pain, I found my rage,
A feral force breaking through the cage.

The cracks deepened, the mold began to fall,
And with it crumbled their rules, their walls.
The shards pierced deep, yet I didn't bleed,
For what broke that day was not what I need.
I stood naked, raw, and unrefined,
No sculptor's hands, just my own mind.
They called me ruined, a hopeless waste,
But I saw freedom in that untamed space.

No longer clay, no longer bound,
I became the earth, solid ground.
And in my chaos, I finally knew,
I was never meant to be shaped by you.
Now, I rise with jagged wings,
A creature of fire, of untold things.
I am not their art; I'm not their plan,
I am my own, both beast and man.

Let them sneer, let them turn away,
I'll walk through storms to find my day.
For breaking free, though it tore me apart,

Was the only way to find my heart

Ripples of Reflection

Breaking free is not a gentle process; it is a tearing, a rending of the soul from everything it has ever known. The mold may feel safe, even comforting, with its clean lines and defined borders, but it is a silent thief, stealing the essence of what lies within. To escape it is to endure a kind of death—not of the body, but of the illusions that once seemed inseparable from identity. The cracks appear slowly at first, barely noticeable, until the pressure becomes unbearable. Each fracture is a moment of anguish, each piece that falls away feels like a piece of life lost.

And yet, with every shattering, something new begins to emerge. There is grief in the destruction, a mourning for the person that was built, even if that person was never truly whole. It is not easy to let go of what once felt like belonging, even when it was a lie. The world outside the mold is vast and terrifying, an expanse filled with the unknown, where there are no boundaries to cling to, no structure to guide the way. The weight of freedom presses heavily, demanding strength that feels impossible to muster. The ache of stepping into this uncharted space is profound, a sorrow that lingers like an old wound.

But in the ruins of the mold, there is a spark—a faint and flickering light that refuses to be extinguished. It is the essence of something real, something unshaped and untamed. This raw, imperfect truth is fragile and wild, defying the constraints that once sought to define it. And it is here, in this chaos, that the soul finds itself again. Not in the perfect symmetry of the mold, but in the jagged edges and the scars that tell a story of resilience. The beauty of breaking free is not in the ease of it, but in the strength it takes to rise from the ashes, to claim a light that no one else can ever dim.

3. Oh mirror..

I stand before the mirror, silent, still,
Its surface gleams, yet it never heals.
It holds my gaze but not my truth,
A thousand whispers my heart conceals.

Who am I in this hollow frame,
A nameless shadow bound by shame?
The eyes that meet mine are weary, worn,
Haunted by dreams that time has torn.
Every inch of glass, a battlefield scar,
The remnants of wars fought from afar.
Each crack, a story of nights I've cried,
Each shard, a piece of me that died.

What do you see, oh cruel reflection?
A stranger drowning in her imperfections?
Or a girl who once danced in summer's glow,
Before life taught her what she should not know?
I trace the lines of my face with care,
Fingers trembling through despair.
The softness once there has turned to stone,
A fortress built to shield what's alone.

The cheeks, once kissed by love and sun,
Now pale, abandoned by everyone.
And the lips—do they even speak my name,
Or are they mute from carrying shame?

How many lies have I told myself here,
To quiet the voices that growl and sneer?
How many masks have I crafted to hide
The girl who's breaking just inside?

They say the mirror never lies,
But it does not speak of how time flies,
How youth dissolves, how hearts decay,
How reflections fade as we lose our way.

Do you remember, oh fragile glass,
The days when I believed I'd last?
When my reflection was soft, unscarred,
A canvas untouched, not yet marred?

Now I stare and see a mosaic of pain,
A patchwork of losses I can't explain.
The mirror shows what I cannot undo—
The echoes of love, the things I outgrew.

I wonder, at times, if I even exist,
Or am I a shadow the world has dismissed?
A flicker of light, too faint to see,

SARGAM SINGH

A voice too soft to claim it's free.

Do you see me, or just what I've been?
The remnants of a soul stretched thin?
I reach to touch, but it doesn't feel,
The reflection's cold, but the wounds so real.

Perhaps the glass is not to blame,
For holding up my fleeting frame.
It cannot speak; it cannot soothe,
It cannot mend what life has bruised.

But still, I search for something more,
A hidden truth, an unlocked door,
Some proof that I am more than this—
A reflection forged from brokenness.

Oh, mirror, keeper of my despair,
Do you see the girl who used to care?
Who laughed at the stars, who danced with the breeze,
Who knelt by the rivers, her soul at ease?

She lingers here, I know she must,
Buried beneath the weight of dust.
And if I dig, if I dare to unearth,
Perhaps I'll find her, my rebirth.

But until that day, I'll stand alone,
Face to face with the girl I've known.

I'll meet her eyes and hold her stare,
Even if what I see is hard to bear.

For maybe the journey is not to mend,
But to embrace what cannot bend.
To love the scars, the cracks, the pain,
And find beauty in what will always remain.

Ripples of Reflection

The mirror is not just an object; it's a confrontation I never asked for. Every glance feels like a conversation with someone I barely recognize—a fragile truce between who I was and who I'm becoming. The reflection stares back, quiet yet deafening, demanding answers I'm not ready to give. Is this who I've always been, or just a version of myself shaped by others' hands? The glass doesn't lie, but it doesn't comfort either. It simply exists, like me, waiting for it's meaning.

The stories etched into my face are ones I didn't choose to write. Each line, each imperfection feels like a scar from battles fought in silence. And yet, I can't look away. There's a strange comfort in the ache, a fragile hope that maybe, somewhere in the cracks, I'll find the person I once was. But how do you search for something when you're not even sure it existed?

I tell myself that the mirror is cruel, but deep down, I know it's not the mirror that wounds me—it's the truth it reflects. The truth of a girl who has worn too many masks, carried too many expectations, and lost too much of herself in the process. And yet, in this quiet, painful stillness, I wonder: is it possible to unearth who I was beneath all the rubble? Or must I build someone entirely new?

4. The Perfection of Imperfection

Beneath the vast, unyielding skies,
Where stars are scattered like endless lies,
The moon ascends, her face marred with scars,
A beacon of beauty among the stars.

She is not flawless, her surface torn,
Her craters whisper of ages worn.
Yet still, we marvel, we stand in awe,
At her imperfect perfection, her silent draw.

The mountains rise with jagged grace,
Their peaks uneven, a fractured face.
The rivers carve with a crooked hand,
A chaos of curves across the land.

The trees are twisted, their branches stray,
Reaching for light in their own crooked way.
The ocean churns, both fierce and wild,
Its waves unbridled, its heart a child.

And yet we humans, with trembling hands,
Try to smooth the edges, reshape the lands.
We polish and prune, we bend and mend,
In search of a flawlessness without end.

We crave perfection, a flawless guise,
Blind to the truth before our eyes.
For in every crack, in every seam,
Lies the essence of life, the pulse of a dream.

The moon wears her craters with quiet pride,
The stars still shine though their light has died.
The rivers sing songs in their crooked flow,
And the mountains stand tall despite the snow.

Perfection is a cruel, elusive flame,
A phantom we chase with tireless shame.
We hide our scars, we mask our pain,
Pretending we're whole, yet hollow remains.

The porcelain face, unmarred, pristine,
Hides the truth of what's unseen.
The heart with cracks, the soul with wear,
Holds the beauty of what we dare.

For it is not in symmetry we thrive,
But in the flaws that keep us alive.
The uneven beats of a mortal heart,
The broken pieces that make us art.

Why do we yearn for the flawless sphere,
When the moon's imperfections bring her near?
Why do we polish what time will erode,
When the roughest paths are the richest road?

Even the stars, with their ancient glow,
Burn with chaos, their tempests show.
Yet we call them perfect, their light divine,
Ignoring the tumult where they shine.

Perhaps it's time to see anew,
That imperfection is what makes us true.
To love the cracks, the dents, the flaws,
To embrace the chaos without pause.

For the moon still glows, though scarred and old,
The mountains rise, untamed and bold.
The rivers carve, the trees still bend,
And the stars still burn until their end.

So let us wear our imperfections loud,
A badge of honor, humble, proud.
For in the imperfect, life takes form,
In the broken, beauty is born.

The pursuit of perfection may tear us apart,
But the cracks are where light enters the heart.
And when we see the truth, we'll know,

That perfection was never ours to bestow.

Ripples of reflection

Perfection is the illusion that binds us, a cruel mirage glimmering on the horizon, forever out of reach. We sculpt our lives as though smoothing every edge and erasing every flaw will grant us transcendence, will make us whole. But look at the moon, luminous in her imperfection, her surface etched with craters that sing of collisions and chaos. She casts her light not despite her scars but because of them. The earth itself is a symphony of flaws—mountains that erupt violently into jagged peaks, rivers that carve crooked paths, leaves that fall in their own imperfect rhythm. And yet, we stand amidst this orchestra of imperfection and demand perfection of ourselves, as if beauty could only exist in what is unmarred, untouched, unbroken.

But what is perfection if not the death of growth? It is in the cracks where the light filters through; it is in the flaws that stories are written. A tree's twisted branches hold the weight of countless storms, and it is in their bends and breaks that their strength resides. The ocean's tide does not smooth every shore but leaves its chaotic signature—shells broken, sand scattered, lines drawn and redrawn. Why, then, do we fear the marks time leaves upon us? Why do we polish and perfect, until all that is raw and real is erased?

The heart does not beat in perfect time; it skips, it falters, it races in moments of love, of loss, of joy. Our laughter is not a melody of precision but bursts of chaos, uncontrollable and pure. The soul itself is a mosaic of shattered moments pieced together, its beauty lying not in symmetry but in the stories each fragment holds. What we call imperfections are the fingerprints of life itself, the proof that we are alive, that we have lived, that we have been touched by the world and have, in turn, touched it back.

To chase perfection is to chase an empty sky, to seek a world stripped of its essence. The moon would not shine without her scars. The earth would not breathe without its wildness. And we, fragile as we are, would not be human without our glorious, messy, beautiful imperfections. Let us abandon the tyranny of flawlessness and embrace the truth that imperfection is not the absence of beauty but its purest form. In our cracks, in our chaos, in our imperfections—we find not only our humanity but the divine spark that makes life worth living.

5. Becoming yourself

In the stillness, when the weight of the world feels like too much,
And the heartache lingers, soft yet sharp—like a tender touch,
There is a moment, just a fleeting breath,
When the past calls louder than the promise of rest.
But even here, in the quiet ache,
A whisper stirs, a pulse, a break.

You are not the sum of the battles you've fought,
Nor the scars etched in shadows, forgotten, caught.
You are not the voice that doubted your grace,
But the quiet strength that refuses to erase.
Each tear, each wound, a verse in your song,
A story of survival, of coming back strong.

The nights may stretch, heavy and long,
When it feels as though everything's gone wrong.
But in that darkness, where silence cries,
A spark ignites in the quietest sighs.
It's not about the force of the fight,
But the gentle resilience to rise with the light.

You've carried the weight of the world on your back,
Yet you've never broken, never lost track.
The strength you've sought was never far away—

It was in the quiet moments you'd pushed aside, day by day.
So let the pain you've known become the grace you carry,
For in your softness, your soul is never contrary.

The path may not be clear, nor easy to trace,
But your heart is a compass, a steady embrace.
And though you may falter, doubt, or fall,
There's a beauty in that—there's no shame at all.
You are the star that hides in the haze,
The quiet flame that lights the maze.

You will rise—not with noise, but with grace,
Not with power, but with a steady pace.
For in the quiet, where the world is still,
You'll find your strength, your heart, your will.
And when the world tries to tell you you're small,
You'll stand with certainty, answering the call.

You'll remember then, as the days unfold,
That every step you took was bold.
Not in grand gestures, not in loud claims,
But in the quiet, where no one knows your name.
You are your own light, your own guiding star,
And even from the furthest, you've come so far.

So when you're weary, when the world's too much to bear,
Know that your spirit, though tired, will repair.
For in the silence of your brokenness, you'll see—
The person you're becoming is the best version to be.

Ripples of Reflection

In the deepest silence, when the weight of all you've carried feels too much to hold, there's a quiet truth you may not yet see. You have been through so much, fought battles you never asked for, and yet here you are, breathing, existing, still moving forward. The world may not have made space for your pain, but you've learned how to carve out your own. In the moments when everything felt shattered, you unknowingly began to rebuild—piece by piece, scar by scar. It's in those fragments that your true power lies, in the parts of you that were never broken, but only hidden from sight. You've been your own warrior all along. And now, it's time to step into the light, not as someone seeking to fit into a mold, but as someone who knows they were always meant to shine. The journey to becoming yourself is not about perfection; it's about knowing that even in your brokenness, you are whole. And in the quiet of your heart, you'll find the strength to rise—again and again, with each new breath.

6. Beyond labels

They didn't ask who you were; they told you instead,
Slapping labels on your soul, like price tags left unsaid,
Discounting your worth before you knew its weight,
Telling you who you should be, sealing your fate.

"Too loud," they hissed, as if your voice could break glass,
"Too quiet," they sneered, like silence was a sin to surpass.
"Too much," they sighed, as if the fire inside
Should shrink to embers, quiet and denied.

You stood still, waiting too long,
Believing their approval was where you belonged.
With each forced smile, each hollow nod,
You betrayed your truth, though they never saw.

The fracture deepened, widening fast,
A rift between who you were, and who they'd cast.
The weight of their vision, the mask you wore,
Pulled you further from yourself, leaving you unsure

In sleepless nights so still, so deep,
Their stories unraveled, denying you sleep.
Their words, you saw, were never your own,

But fears they carried, seeds they'd sown.

Failures hidden, control they sought,
To bind the chaos your brilliance brought.
Yet through their echoes, your truth took flight,
For none could dim your untamed light.

And then, within a breathless pause,
You questioned all their fleeting laws:
"Without their tales, what truth is mine?
What lies beyond their fragile design?"

The answer whispered, slow, unsure,
A path of fragments to endure.
With trembling hands, you tore the seams,
Unraveling doubts and borrowed dreams.

The ache was fierce, but you endured,
Stretching to form a self assured.
A shape reborn, your light reclaimed,
Untouched by stories they had framed.

And when the weight began to fall,
It didn't shatter, not at all.
It softly dissolved, a fleeting haze,
Like fog that fades in the morning's gaze.

What lay beneath was strange, unknown,
Raw and unpolished, yet your own.

No longer bound by borrowed lore,
You found yourself, and something more.

You are the poet,
The ink that flows,
The page where untamed beauty grows.
You are the silence they cannot quell,
The boundless horizon they'll never spell.
So let them keep their labels tight,
Call you wild, call you night.
Call you wrong, too much, too small—
Their labels crumble, that's all.

For their words are but fading echoes,
Lost in the depth where your spirit grows.
You stand, unmarked, a force unknown,
A soul that's finally all its own.

For you are not a mold to be filled,
but a river carving its own path.
Not a shadow cast by their light,
but a sun rising in its own time.

And if they dare ask who you are,
you'll answer with a smile that holds the universe,
and say,
"I am everything I was meant to be.
I am free."

Ripples of Reflection

They will pull at the threads of your spirit, stretching you thin, trying to bend you into something you are not, something they need you to be. The world will whisper its demands—soft at first, then louder, until it roars through every corner of your soul, drowning out the quiet parts of you that long for truth. They will tell you who you should love, how you should act, what you should say, until you start to forget the sound of your own voice. They'll hand you a mirror that shows only the parts of yourself they want to see, and in its reflection, you may lose sight of the person who was always meant to be. But in the stillness, in the silence beneath their words, you will hear it: the beating of your heart, the hum of your own existence, untouched by their gaze. In those moments when you feel lost, when the weight of their vision presses down upon you, remember that there is more than what they see, more than what they demand. You are not bound by their definitions, nor their limitations. You are an untamed force, a song that has yet to be fully sung, a fire that refuses to be extinguished. They will try to reshape you, to make you fit, to tame your wildness, but the truth is: you cannot be contained. You are the tempest and the calm, the night and the day, the dream and the waking. And one day, when the dust settles, when the noise of their judgments fades, you will stand in your own light, free from their chains, free from their labels.

You will remember who you are, and you will know that their words no longer have power over you. You are not theirs to define. You are yours to discover. And that is a truth no one can take from you.

• 29 •

7. Scars and Starlight

The moon, pale and weary, wears its scars like a crown,
A silent sovereign of the sky, looking gently down.
It hangs in solitude, yet commands the seas,
A guardian of secrets whispered in the breeze.
Stars scatter like shattered glass across velvet skies,
Each a fragment of a wish, a prayer that never dies.
They burn with quiet fire, distant yet near,
Echoing the hopes we cradle—and the fears we bear.

Beneath their vigil, the waves rise in song,
A ceaseless rhythm, unyielding, strong.
They rush to meet the shore with eager embrace,
Only to retreat, as if ashamed of their place.

Are we not the same as the restless sea?
Racing toward something we're desperate to be.
Crashing forward, breaking, and pulling away,
Carrying fragments of dreams we can never quite say.

The moon sees it all but speaks not a word,
Its silence a comfort, a truth unheard.
For it knows the ache of being alone,
Yet it shines, resilient, on its celestial throne.

The stars above, unblinking, persist,
Proof that even in distance, we exist.
They remind us: light doesn't falter with time,
It endures the void, steadfast and sublime.

The waves—they whisper what hearts cannot tell,
Of battles fought quietly, of times we fell.
But they sing, too, of rising, of relentless might,
Of finding beauty in darkness, of forging light.

Look to the moon, and see your own face,
A reflection of strength in the coldest of space.
Gaze at the stars, and know you belong,
To a tapestry vast, to a symphony's song.
The waves will remind you: breaking's no sin,
It's the way the ocean reshapes from within.
In every retreat, there's a chance to begin,
A rhythm reborn, a new song to spin.

And so, let the cosmos cradle your soul,
Let the tides teach you of feeling whole.
For in the moon's scars, the stars' quiet glow,
And the waves' wild dance, the truth will show.

We are fragments of chaos, yet part of a plan,
Connected to every star, wave, and span.
A fleeting existence, yet infinite, free,
A drop in the ocean, yet the whole sea.

The tides carry stories, etched in salt and sand,
Of dreams forgotten, yet held in their hand.
Each crest, each fall, is a tale retold,
Of love once lost, of courage bold.

The moonlight spills like silver rain,
Washing the edges of sorrow and pain.
It doesn't heal, but it lets us see,
The beauty in scars, in what's meant to be.

Stars sing softly, a lullaby of the night,
Promising peace in their flickering light.
They whisper, "You're vast as the sky we adorn,
A mosaic of storms and skies reborn."

And as the waves kiss the moonlit shore,
They remind you: there's always more.
More to feel, to break, to mend,
A cycle eternal, where nothing ends.

Ripples of reflection

The moon, scarred and luminous, gazes down like a silent confidant, holding secrets older than time itself. Its light spills across the restless waves, reflecting their fury and grace, as if to say, "I see you." The stars, distant and fierce, burn themselves into eternity, offering a reminder that even in destruction, there is brilliance. We stand beneath this infinite dome, overwhelmed by its grandeur, and yet, we carry the audacity to believe we are unworthy. Why do we shrink in the face of what we are also made of? The tides crash forward and pull back, unashamed of their longing, unafraid of their retreat. And here we are, shaming ourselves for wanting too much, for not being enough, for breaking and rebuilding in a way that only we can understand.

But the universe doesn't scorn us—it holds us. It whispers through the wind and the waves, reminding us that we are no less miraculous than the constellations etched into the night. The sky is not silent; it sings of resilience, of survival, of the beauty in our imperfections. If the moon can wear its scars with pride, if the stars can burn without apology, why do we dull our own light for fear of being seen?

Perhaps the chaos within us is not a flaw but a story—a rhythm in tune with the dance of the cosmos. Like the tides that rise and fall, we are allowed to falter, to ebb, to find ourselves in the quiet moments before the next surge. We are not meant to be still; we are meant to shift and sway, to carry the pull of what's beyond us and the weight of what's within. And when the darkness threatens to consume us, remember: even the moon glows brightest in the night. Your light, your struggle, your story—it all matters. You are a tide, a star, a moon, a universe contained within a single, fragile human heartbeat. Feel it. Own it. Let it shine.

8. Whispers in the void

There is a stillness, deep and unspoken,
A quiet that carries weight, like the final breath
Of a world that has screamed its sorrows,
Only to be silenced by the vastness of space.

It is the silence after the storm's violent rage,
When thunder no longer cracks the sky,
And the wind's howls are nothing more than a memory.
In this stillness, the universe takes a breath,
And so do you.

You stand there, in the aftermath,
Surrounded by the soft hum of life continuing—
But you feel separate from it all,
As if you are floating, suspended in this moment,
Caught between who you were before,
And who you are yet to be.

The world is silent, yet your thoughts are louder than ever.
It is the silence of realization,
That you have survived, but at what cost?

The night is no longer an abyss;
It is a canvas, stretched wide,

Waiting for the first stroke of dawn,
But until then, you stand beneath a sky
Full of stars that do not answer,
Not yet.

They twinkle like fleeting promises,
Like the half-formed dreams you can never quite catch.
You try to listen to the silence,
To let it speak, to let it show you the way,
But all you hear is the echo of your own longing,
Whispering things you are too afraid to face.

You ache for meaning in this silence,
Like a child reaching for the moon—
It's there, just out of reach,
But you can't help but stretch your hands to the sky,
As if somehow, it will answer,
As if somehow, it will fill the emptiness.
But the silence only deepens,

Like the space between two souls,
Both yearning, both unsure,
And yet, both too proud to speak.

Still, there is beauty in the silence,
A beauty that cuts deep,
A beauty that doesn't need to be spoken,
But felt in the bones, in the cracks of your heart,
Where the storm once raged, and now,
Only the quiet remains.

The world may press its weight on your shoulders,
But in this moment, you find peace—
Not in the answers,
But in the willingness to remain,
To stand still in the face of uncertainty,
And let the stillness fill you up,
Until it becomes a part of you.

For it is in the quiet that you find yourself,
Not in the roar of the world,
But in the soft, steady pulse of your own breath.
In the silence, you are not lost—
You are becoming,
A whispered promise in the dark,
A seed in the soil,
Waiting for the sun to rise,
But knowing that the night, too,

Has its place in your journey.

The world may spin,
But in this moment, you are still.
The storm has passed,
And you are here,
Not broken, but healed—
Not empty, but full of the things you never knew you needed.
And in the quiet, you begin to hear the truth,
Not in the noise, but in the space between.

It is not the storm that defines you,
But the stillness that follows.
And in that silence, you find your strength,
Not the strength to fight,
But the strength to simply be,
To exist, to breathe, to wait,
And to know that in the quiet,
You are whole.

Ripples of Reflection

In the moments when the world falls silent, when the clamor of voices and the rush of life come to a halt, you are left alone with your thoughts, fragile and vulnerable. The air is thick with the weight of all that has been left unsaid, and the stillness feels like a heavy blanket, pressing down on you, suffocating yet oddly comforting. You sit in the quiet, surrounded by memories that refuse to fade, each one a ghost of the past, haunting the very corners of your mind. In this stillness, time seems to slow, stretching endlessly, and you begin to wonder if it has always been this way—or if it is you who has changed, becoming more attuned to the silence that once felt so foreign, so unbearable.

But in this pause, you find something unexpected—clarity. Like the first breath after a storm, it is sharp and cleansing, cutting through the layers of confusion that once clouded your heart. There, in the midst of the silence, you see the truth of who you are. You see the brokenness, yes, but you also see the resilience that has been hidden in the quiet spaces of your soul. The weight of the world might have pressed down on you, but in this stillness, you are reminded that it has not crushed you. You have not been destroyed by the silence; you have been shaped by it.

And so, you sit with it, allowing the silence to become your teacher, your guide. In the absence of noise, you find a strange comfort, a deep knowing that you are not alone in your solitude. Every whispered thought, every fragile hope that surfaces in the quiet moments, is a piece of your truth, a part of the journey that you are on. The silence, though deafening, is not empty; it is filled with all that you need to heal, to grow, to move forward.

It is in these moments of quiet introspection that you find your strength—not in the loud declarations of victory, but in the soft, steady rhythm of your heartbeat, the pulse of life that refuses to fade. And you realize, with a quiet awe, that the answers you seek are not outside of you, but within. The silence is not a void to fear, but a space of profound possibility, where you can rediscover yourself, rebuild your broken pieces, and emerge stronger than before. It is in the stillness that you learn to embrace the parts of yourself you have long ignored, to forgive the wounds that have festered, and to finally give yourself the grace you have always denied. For in this quiet, you are not lost—you are simply becoming. And when the silence eventually lifts, you will not be the same person who entered it. You will be whole.

9. A Lie Carved in Stone

They said forever like it was carved in stone,
A sacred hymn, a truth well-known.
But forever is a whisper, a fleeting breeze,
A shadow that dances but never sees.

You held their words as though they were light,
Guiding you gently through the endless night.
But stars can fall, and so did their vow,
Leaving you stranded in the here and now.

The touch that once lingered has faded to air,
The promises made now too heavy to bear.
Their laughter, a ghost in the halls of your mind,
A cruel reminder of what's left behind.

Forever, they said, with a smile so sweet,
As if the earth wouldn't crumble beneath your feet.
But time, the thief, with its callous hand,
Unraveled the dreams like a line in the sand.

You built your world on their gentle lies,
A fragile kingdom beneath fleeting skies.
Each word they spoke, a thread in your soul,
Now frayed and broken, leaving you less than whole.

Did they know that forever could shatter so fast?
That love could dissolve like a spell never cast?
Or were they just a mirror, reflecting your fears,
Disappearing into the blur of your tears?

The nights are quieter, the air too still,
The ache in your chest refuses to fill.
You trace the cracks of your breaking heart,
Trying to find where it fell apart.

Yet somewhere amidst the rubble and pain,
A quiet truth begins to reign:
Forever was never theirs to give—
It's a fleeting myth, not where we live.

For moments are all we're truly owed,
Brief sparks of light before they erode.
And though the echoes of love may lie,
The courage to feel will never die.

You are the bearer of stories untold,
A heart that beats, both fierce and bold.
Forever may falter, but you remain,
Rising like the sun after the rain.

So grieve the loss, let the tears run free,
Mourn what was and what could never be.
But know that forever is not the end—
It's the lessons learned, the wounds that mend.

For in the silence, you'll hear your name,
Not as a victim of love's cruel game,
But as a warrior, standing tall,
Who dared to love, to risk it all.

Forever is a lie, but life is true—
A story rewritten, starting anew.
You carry the pieces, the love, the ache,
And with every step, new paths you'll make.

So let them say forever—let them pretend.
You know it's moments, not forever, that mend.
And when they ask how you survived the goodbye,

You'll smile and say, "Because I learned to fly."

Ripples of reflection

Forever—it's the sweetest lie we tell ourselves, the cruelest hope we cling to, the softest dagger that cuts the deepest. We wrap it around promises, thread it into vows, weave it into the fabric of our dreams, believing that something so fragile could withstand the storms of time. But forever was never meant to be kind. It was a fleeting spark, a moment disguised as eternity, and we—naïve, desperate, hopelessly human—held it too tightly, crushed it with the weight of our longing.

When forever fades, it doesn't scream; it slips through your fingers in silence, like sand carried by a quiet wind. You feel it in the spaces left behind—in the hollow sound of a name unspoken, in the phantom touch of a hand no longer there. You feel it in the echo of a laugh that once filled the air, in the shadows of what could have been. And the world doesn't stop; it doesn't mourn with you. It moves on, cold and indifferent, while you sit in the ruins, trying to piece together the shards of what you thought was unbreakable.

But perhaps the lie of forever is not in its promise, but in how we understand it. Forever isn't a destination; it's a fleeting moment, a whispered truth wrapped in the chaos of now. It's the way their eyes looked at you that one perfect evening, the way your heart raced when you first dared to believe. Forever isn't in the years that follow or the memories that linger; it's in the seconds that felt infinite because they were shared with someone who made time stand still.

And when forever crumbles, we are left not with nothing, but with everything. The ache, the love, the loss—they become the threads of a new story, one we didn't want but one we needed. We carry pieces of forever in our hearts, fragments of a world we built in the image of love, fragments that remind us that even the most fleeting connections can leave marks that last a lifetime.

So if forever was a lie, let it be the most beautiful lie we ever told. Let it be the reason we loved recklessly, without reservation. Let it be the reason we dared to hope, dared to dream, dared to lose. And in the end, let it teach us that the truth of forever lies not in its promise, but in the courage to embrace the fleeting moments that make us whole.

10. Chains Beneath Velvet

"To those who believe the grass on the other side isn't always greener,
dare to cross over—you might just find it adorned with flowers!"

They drew the lines before your first breath,
Charted the path from cradle to death.
With tender smiles and whispered care,
They built you a world, but it was so unfair.

"You belong here," they gently lied,
While locking the door and standing outside.
The walls they raised were cloaked in love,
Yet felt like thorns in a velvet glove.

"Not too loud, not too wild," they said,
"Hold your tongue, lower your head."
Every step you took was measured and weighed,
Every dream a debt you silently paid.

"Be kind, be soft, but don't ask why,"
"Stay on the ground, don't aim for the sky."
But how can a flame burn fierce and true,
When told its light must dim, subdued?

The world outside shimmered, vast and free,
A song you hummed but couldn't see.
The stars called out with a radiant glow,
Yet you were told, "It's better not to know."

For every boundary they set in stone,
Became the bars of a prison you'd own.
You danced within their narrow frame,
A puppet twisting to a nameless shame.

And when you dared to step too near,
To the edge of their comfort, the brink of their fear,
The silence would fall, heavy and cold,
A warning wrapped in the guise of gold.

They told you, "It's love, it's for your good,"
But love shouldn't suffocate where it stood.
It shouldn't clip wings that ache to fly,
Or turn freedom into a hushed goodbye.

Your soul rebelled in quiet despair,
A bird with a song too heavy to share.
In the midnight hours, alone in your mind,
You dreamt of a place they'd never define.
A place where you could stumble and fall,
Without the fear of losing it all.

Where laughter could echo wild and untamed,
And tears could flow without being shamed.

The cage they built was gilded, fine,
With bars that glimmered and seemed benign.
But even gold can weigh you down,
A shimmering mask for chains that drown.

For every time you tried to explain,
They brushed it off as childish pain.
"Someday, you'll thank us," they'd softly insist,
As if their control was a gift you'd missed.

Yet deep within, your spirit grew,
A quiet storm, defiant and true.
It whispered of rivers that carved their own way,
Of mountains that dared to greet the day.

It reminded you that the stars don't ask,
For permission to shine, or wear a mask.
And neither should you, with your untamed fire,
Your boundless depth, your unyielding desire.

One day, the walls will crumble, fall,
And you'll step beyond their narrow hall.
The weight will lift, the air will clear,
And you'll embrace the truth you hold dear.

That boundaries may shape, but they can't define,
The infinite strength that is wholly mine.
And in that moment, when you stand alone,
Under skies uncharted, wholly your own,
You'll realize freedom was never theirs to give,
It was always your birthright—your reason to live.

Ripples of reflection

The boundaries we grow within are often invisible to those who set them—a fortress built not from malice but from fear disguised as care. Each line drawn, each rule whispered, claims to protect but often confines, leaving behind a trail of unspoken longing. How do you explain the ache of a heart that yearns for horizons it has never seen? How do you mourn the life you might have lived, had you been given the space to wander freely? Boundaries promise safety, but they come at the cost of wings clipped before they've ever taken flight. They tether dreams to the earth, turning aspirations into whispers of what could have been. Yet even within those confines, the soul stirs, restless, carving cracks in the walls and letting fragments of light seep in. And in those fragments lies the truth: no boundary, no matter how strong, can contain the infinite within.

11. Waltz of Light and Shadow

In the quiet recess of the heart's deep core,
Where shadows stretch and the wild winds roar,
Hope and doubt collide, forever at war,
A dance of light and dark we can't ignore.

Hope rises like the dawn, full of grace,
A beacon that lights the darkest space.
It speaks to our souls, urging us to rise,
To reach for the stars, to claim the skies.

But doubt is the shadow that whispers low,
A chilling voice that seeks to slow
Our every step, our every stride,
It tells us the dreams are just too wide.

Hope is the flame that burns in the night,
It gives us courage, it gives us sight,
A light that flickers but never fades,
A promise of joy in the coldest shades.

But doubt is the chill, the freezing breeze,
It gnaws at our bones, it brings us to our knees,
It feeds on our fear, it grows with time,
It wraps around us, like a rhythmless rhyme.

Hope is the river that flows to the sea,
It carries us forward, it sets us free.
A current of strength, it pulls us on,
Singing of futures and a brighter dawn.

But doubt is the weight that sinks our boat,
A storm that crashes, a sinking note,
It pushes us downward, it makes us fall,
It tells us, "You're too small for it all."

Hope is the star that flickers above,
It shines with the promise of endless love,
A glimmer of light in a world of gray,
It whispers, "Keep moving, you'll find your way."

But doubt is the fog that clouds our view,
It blurs the path, it hides what's true,
It speaks in riddles, it twists the mind,
It leaves us searching, but nothing to find.

Hope is the mountain that rises so high,
It beckons us upward, it touches the sky,
It tells us, "Climb higher, don't you despair,
You're meant for greatness, your soul will bear."

But doubt is the valley, dark and deep,
It pulls us under, it makes us weep,
It tells us to stop, it whispers, "You can't,"
It wraps us in chains, it holds us in a chant.

Hope is the promise of all that can be,
A vision of life, so wild and so free,
It sings of tomorrow, it dreams of today,
It fills us with fire, and keeps us at bay.

But doubt is the prison, the silent wall,
It closes us in, it makes us small,
It dims our fire, it snuffs our flame,
It tells us, "You're nothing, just play the game."

Hope is the sunrise, breaking the dark,
A signal of new beginnings, a fresh start,
It tells us, "This day, it's yours to win,"
It whispers of joy, it calls from within.

But doubt is the night, the endless black,
A shadow that pulls, a constant attack,
It says, "You are weak, you'll never make it,"
It pushes us back, it makes us forsake it.

Hope is the music, the song we can hear,
It fills us with love, it chases the fear,
It tells us to dance, to laugh, to sing,

It speaks of the beauty in everything.

But doubt is the silence, the deafening roar,
The echo of failure that rings at the door,
It tells us we're nothing, it seals the sound,
It keeps us from dancing, it keeps us from ground.

Hope is the answer that calls from the deep,
It speaks of the dreams we're destined to keep,
It says, "You are strong, you're meant for this fight,"
It tells us we're worthy, it shines so bright.

But doubt is the question that we cannot ignore,
The one that keeps asking, "What's it all for?"
It fills us with worry, it clouds our mind,
It traps us in circles, it's never kind.

Hope is the road that stretches ahead,
A path of potential, of things unsaid,
It tells us, "The journey is worth the cost,"
It gives us a reason, no matter what's lost.

But doubt is the shadow that lingers behind,
It holds us in place, it twists what we find,
It says, "Don't move forward, don't take the leap,"
It pulls us back down into the deep.

Hope is the love that burns in the soul,
It keeps us alive, it makes us whole,

It says, "You can do it, you can achieve,"
It tells us to trust, to believe, to believe.

But doubt is the fear that binds the heart tight,
It makes us question, it dims the light,
It says, "You will fail, you will lose,"
It makes us afraid of what we might choose.

Hope is the dream that fills up the night,
It calls us to chase, to take flight,
It fills us with hope, it opens the door,
It says, "You are worthy of so much more."

But doubt is the chain that keeps us in place,
It tells us we're nothing, it says, "You can't face
The trials ahead, the challenges tall,"
It drags us down with every fall.

And so, we dance between both with grace,
Caught in the rhythm of a never-ending race,
Hope pulls us forward, doubt tugs us back,
We fight for the future, but get lost in the track.

Hope whispers softly, a melody sweet,
Telling us to move, to rise, to meet
The world that awaits, with arms open wide,
It says, "You can conquer, don't you hide."

But doubt screams louder, a thunderous sound,
It tells us to stop, to not make a sound,
It makes us question what's truly right,
It fills our hearts with endless fright.

So we dance, between hope and doubt,
A never-ending cycle, a constant rout,
Chasing a dream, caught in the fray,
Fighting the battle, day after day.

Ripples of reflection

Beneath the weight of a sky that stretches infinitely, where the stars twinkle like fragile promises, there lies a space—a space between what we are and what we could be, suspended in time, suspended in doubt. The tides of our hopes crash against the shores of our fears, each wave louder than the last, pulling us deeper into the unknown, yet we stand at the edge, gazing into the horizon that never quite promises an answer. In the quiet moments when we are left alone with our thoughts, we feel the tug of the world pulling us one way and our heart pulling us the other. It is a constant dance, a waltz between the moon's reassuring glow and the darkness that lingers just beyond. We tell ourselves to be brave, to leap into the unknown with the confidence of stars, yet our feet are shackled by the invisible weight of uncertainty, each step forward burdened by a question we cannot quite ask.

In this space, we are all caught, caught between the fervor of our dreams and the crushing weight of our doubts. There are times when hope burns brighter than the sun, and we feel invincible, as though nothing could ever extinguish the fire inside us. But then there are the moments, the quiet, still moments, when doubt creeps in, wrapping its cold fingers around our hearts and dimming the light we thought would never fade. These are the moments that make us question everything, the moments when the path ahead seems too uncertain, the dreams too distant, and the fear too consuming. Yet, even in that silence, there remains a spark—a tiny, flickering light that refuses to go out. It whispers to us, gently reminding us that we have stood here before, at this very crossroads, and found our way through the fog.

We are constantly at war with ourselves, torn between the light that guides us and the shadows that threaten to consume us. And in the midst of this struggle, there is beauty—imperfect, fleeting, yet undeniable. It is the beauty of knowing that even in our darkest moments, we are still capable of reaching for something greater than ourselves. The dance between hope and doubt is not a battle to be won, but a rhythm to be embraced, a melody we must learn to play, no matter how out of tune we feel. For every step we take in the face of uncertainty, every moment we hold on to our dreams despite the weight of the world, we find something new within ourselves. Something strong, something enduring, something that will carry us through the storms, even when the sky seems too heavy to bear.

This space, this in-between, is where we grow. It is where we learn to trust the journey, even when we cannot see the destination. For in the dance between hope and doubt, there is a grace that only those who have dared to dream can understand.

12. Echoes of a Dying Star

Fear weaves itself beneath the fabric of my skin,
An ancient hymn, a battle I never asked to begin.
It lurks in the marrow, where silence resides,
A predator pacing in shadows, where courage hides.

My heart, a trembling prisoner in its cage,
Beats a rhythm of terror, a dance of rage.
Each pulse a cry, a plea to the stars,
A desperate whisper to heal these scars.

The moon, a pale voyeur in the velvet sky,
Watches as fear turns my dreams awry.
Its light grazes my trembling frame,
Softly illuminating my unspoken shame.

Lungs that should fill with the breath of night
Instead quiver beneath fear's relentless bite.
They inhale shards of the coldest air,
And exhale despair, a silent prayer.

My hands, shaking maps of fragile veins,
Hold the echoes of yesterday's pains.
They reach for constellations that feel too far,
Grasping at fragments of a dying star.

My skin, a parchment etched with dread,
Carries the weight of words unsaid.
It stretches thin over bones that ache,
A vessel for sorrow, a fragile lake.

Eyes that once marveled at celestial grace
Now reflect the shadows etched on my face.
They trace the arcs of the heavens above,
Searching for answers in starlit love.

The stars, eternal witnesses to human plight,
Hold their silent vigil through the night.
They watch as fear consumes my flame,
A thief that leaves only a hollow name.

The earth beneath me whispers low,
A grounding voice in the ebb and flow.

"Fear is a shadow, fleeting and slight,
A trick of the mind in the absence of light."

But fear is no shadow, no fleeting ghost,
It is the beast I feed the most.
It gnaws at my thoughts, my fleeting joys,
Turning moments of silence into deafening noise.

The waves of my mind rise high and wild,
Crashing over the innocence of the child
That once dreamed of mountains, stars, and flight,
Now clings to the ground in trembling fright.

The moon wanes, yet whispers still,
"Let fear bend you, but not your will.
For every star that falls from grace
Leaves behind a trail, a luminous trace."

I am not the storm, though it roars within,
I am not the shadows that dance on my skin.
I am the stillness that comes with the dawn,
The quiet resolve to keep moving on.

Fear, though vast, is not my whole,
It cannot possess what lies in my soul.
For within the cosmos, beneath the despair,
Lies a strength that no fear can impair.

So let the moon witness, let the stars see,
That even in fear, I am boundlessly free.
Let the earth feel my trembling, my cries,
For in every fall, the phoenix must rise.

• • •

Fear will falter, its hold will break,
A fleeting shadow that I'll forsake.
And as the stars weave light through my scars,
I'll stand unshaken beneath their eternal memoirs.

Ripples of reflection

Fear is a ghost that lingers in the chambers of the soul, pressing its icy fingers against the heart, making it beat too fast or not at all. It slips beneath the skin, crawling like a silent predator, carving doubts into flesh that longs to heal. It whispers in the quiet hours when the world is asleep, its voice mingling with the rustle of leaves and the hum of distant stars. It is the weight behind trembling hands, the shadow behind hesitant steps, the storm behind eyes that refuse to meet their own reflection.

It takes the form of the night, vast and unending, swallowing the horizon and veiling the moon in a haze of uncertainty. It feeds on the unknown, grows in the spaces where questions are too painful to ask. Fear does not shatter loudly; it erodes quietly, like waves wearing down the edges of a once-proud cliff. It convinces us that the darkness is infinite, that the stars are too distant to reach, that our voices will only echo into emptiness.

But fear is not the end; it is a beginning masked in dread. Beneath its suffocating layers lies a seed of something greater. The heart, though bruised, remembers how to beat for hope. The skin, though marked by fear's passage, learns to stretch toward warmth and light. The trembling hands begin to steady, not because fear vanishes, but because we learn to carry it without letting it steer us.

Even in the deepest dark, the stars remain. Even in the quietest moments of despair, there is the hum of life, a pulse that defies the silence. Fear may root itself in us, but so too does courage, waiting patiently to bloom. And as we face the night, we learn to weave our own constellations, to find strength in the cracks fear has left behind. It is in these fractures, these moments of stillness and confrontation, that we become more than we were—whole, in a way we never imagined possible.

· 65 ·

13. Tides of Silent Strength

The river begins in silence, unnoticed,
A whisper between the stones and trees,
It has no name, no reason, no purpose—
It simply follows the path of the breeze.
A pulse, an instinct, a force that flows,
It moves without thought, where no one knows.

In the quiet of the morning, the river listens,
To the secrets the earth holds, still and deep,
Every bend carved by the hands of time,
A map of tears that the heavens weep.
The rocks beneath it—steady, unyielding—
They have watched the river change, and never feel the sting.

The water meets the mountains, high and proud,
But it does not stop, it does not bow.
It carries the weight of ancient fears,
The echoes of storms, of lost years.
Its path is shaped by forces unseen,
A dance with the sky, a vision serene.

Each ripple on the surface tells a tale,
Of hearts that broke and hopes that failed,
Of whispered promises that couldn't last,

Of memories trapped in a rushing past.
Yet, still it moves, relentless, undeterred,
With every wave, a new thought stirred.

The river, though burdened by its pain,
Finds beauty in the journey—again and again.
It carves through forests, unseen and unknown,
Pushing onward to places it's never been shown.
It doesn't mourn, it doesn't regret,
For each new step is a dream unmet.

And then, there are moments—still and quiet—
When the river rests beneath the moon's light.
It lingers in the calm of the night,
But the call to move is always in sight.
A deep yearning in its soft, dark flow,
To reach the sea, to let it go.

It learns to bend, to curve, to break,
To flow through lands that time forsake.
The river carries dreams of its own,
Of shores unseen, of hearts unknown.
It is not the same as it was at birth,
But each new part is a testament to its worth.

Through cities of glass, through fields of gold,
Through skies that weep and winds that fold,
It carries within it all the tears—
The joys, the pains, the unspoken fears.
It knows the taste of salt, of rain,
And it learns that there's no such thing as pain without gain.

And then, the river meets the ocean's arms,
A vast embrace that holds no harm.
It surrenders all, and yet feels free—
The end of a journey, the start of eternity.
The river knows it's come full circle,
A journey complete, a heart unburdened.

But what does the river leave behind?
It leaves the whispers of time entwined,
In every drop that once had flown—
In every lesson, in every stone.
For a journey is not just about the end,
But the paths we take, the hearts we mend.

And when it finally rests in the ocean's depth,
The river knows it has known the breadth—
Of life, of love, of joy and sorrow,
Of what it means to face tomorrow.
For though its waters now dissolve into the sea,
It was never just a river—it was always free.

Ripples of reflection

There are times when the world feels too loud, when every step echoes in a space that seems too vast, too empty to be filled. In those moments, we stand at the crossroads of who we've been and who we're meant to become. The choices we've made, the words we've swallowed, and the silences we've kept weigh on us like the deepest night sky, stretching endlessly, leaving us to wonder whether we'll ever find the courage to shine through. The stories we've carried with us, the masks we've worn to survive, sometimes make us forget the person we were before the world whispered its demands. But deep within, beneath the layers of what we've been taught to be, there's a part of us that still dares to dream, to hope, to break free from the confines of a world that never asked us who we were before it started to define us. This journey—this search for meaning—is not just a battle against the voices of others; it's a battle with the quiet echo of our own doubts. Yet, even as we stand in the shadows of our fears, we are reminded that even the darkest night cannot last forever. And perhaps, it's not about the destination we're heading toward, but the strength we find in simply choosing to walk—one foot after the other, step by step—no matter how broken, no matter how unsure. In the midst of this chaos, there is beauty in the struggle, in the resilience that rises, unnoticed by most, but felt in every breath we take.

14. Fettered Heart, Forgotten Art

Beneath the heavens stretched wide and deep,
Where stars hang heavy in their endless sleep,
I stood, a figure bound in despair,
A bird with wings but chained by air.

The moon, a witness, serene and wise,
Reflected the grief in my hollowed eyes.
Its glow revealed what words could not,
A joy once vibrant, now forgot.

For once, there was a child in me,
A soul as wild as the untamed sea.
She danced with shadows, she chased the sun,
And laughed with the stars when day was done.

Her voice was music, her steps a dream,
Her world alive with colors unseen.
The dawn was hers, the dusk her play,
Every moment a bright array.

Her heart was light, unburdened, free,
But now she whispers reproachfully:
"Where have you gone, the one I knew,
Who painted the world in every hue?

You traded wonder for measured steps,
For chains of logic and cautious depth.
The skies you loved are just a view,
A backdrop now, not a world for you."

Each rib a cage for the echoes within,
Her voice, a lament of what might have been.
I hear her laughter, but it's laced with grief,
A haunting sound, so sharp, so brief.

The winds, they call, with tales untold,
Of lands uncharted, of hearts turned bold.
But my feet are anchored, my spirit restrained,
By invisible threads, meticulously chained.

The rivers carved their relentless trails,
While I stood bound, lost in details.
Their waters whispered, "Let yourself flow,
The world expands when you let go."

The mountains watched, their peaks aloof,
Guardians of wisdom, silent proof.
"Climb," they said, "though steep and bare,
The view you seek is waiting there."

The child I was, the joy she bore,
Now lingers in shadows, a ghost at my core.
She pleads with me to rise once more,
To unshackle my heart and let it soar.

But voices surround me, cold and severe,
Demanding I tread with constant fear.
"Think again," they warn, "Do not misstep,
A moment's error could cost what's kept."

The stars above, once my trusted guide,
Now feel distant, lost, denied.
They shimmer faintly, as if to say,
"The chains you wear are not the way."

The trees lean close, their roots entwined,
Urging me to reclaim my mind.
"Even the strongest must learn to bend,
For rigid branches will never ascend."

The rain, it falls with rhythmic grace,
Each drop a tear, a soft embrace.
"Cleanse yourself," it whispers low,
"Release the weight, and let life flow."

The sun arises, fierce and bright,
It burns away the lingering night.
"Look within," its rays implore,

"You are the warmth you've searched for."

I ache to tell my younger self,
That joy is not confined to wealth.
That dreams need not be boxed or still,
That wonder bends to the strongest will.

But the child in me just shakes her head,
And mourns the life I've left for dead.
"Why must you stifle the fire inside?
Why do you run when you should stride?"

Her eyes pierce mine, a mirror so true,
Reflecting the life I once deeply knew.
"I am still here," her whisper remains,
"Buried beneath these self-made chains."

One day, I swear, the chains will break,
The shadows will lift, the earth will quake.
The skies will open, the stars will sing,
And I will rise on unbroken wings.

The child I lost will take my hand,
We'll roam together, reclaim the land.
For joy is a spark that never fades,
A flame that endures, no matter the shades.

And as the heavens stretch wide and deep,
The stars no longer in endless sleep,

I'll dance again, with shadows and sun,
For my journey back to joy has begun.

Ripples of reflection

In the delicate folds of memory and longing, there exists a space where time stands still—a place where the echoes of childhood laughter meet the relentless weight of growing up. It's a cruel paradox, this journey we're forced to take, where innocence is traded for understanding, and wonder is sacrificed at the altar of practicality. I think of the girl I used to be—the one who saw shapes in the clouds and believed the stars could hear her whispers. She lived with a heart unguarded, fearless in its pursuit of joy, trusting the world to catch her if she fell. But somewhere along the way, the cracks began to show. The world did not catch her; it taught her to build walls instead. And so, brick by brick, layer by layer, I buried her under expectations and doubt, under the constant hum of "be better, do more, think first."

Yet, she's still there, buried but alive, haunting the quiet corners of my soul. Her laughter, once light and unrestrained, now trembles with an unfamiliar sadness. Her eyes, which once reflected the boundless sky, seem to peer at me from some distant place, asking questions I cannot answer. "Why did you let me go?" she seems to say. "Why did you trade dreams for fears, wonder for caution?" I want to tell her that I had no choice, that this is what the world demands—that to grow up is to let go of the child within. But even as I think it, I know it's a lie. Growing up does not have to mean growing cold, and yet, here I am, a stranger to my own heart.

The world I once found magical now feels muted, its edges sharp and unforgiving. The stars, once my confidants, now feel distant, their light too faint to guide me. Even the moon, in its eternal wisdom, seems to pity me, casting its glow not as comfort but as a reminder of all I've lost. And still, there is a part of me that refuses to surrender, a fragment of the girl I once was, fighting against the chains I've wrapped around her. She whispers to me in the dead of night, urging me to remember, to feel, to believe again in the beauty of unguarded joy.

But it's not that simple, is it? To unlearn fear, to dismantle walls, to trust again in the uncertain. The voices around me—the ones that demand perfection, caution, restraint—are loud and persistent, drowning out the gentle hum of my forgotten self. And yet, even as they press in, even as they weigh me down, I feel the faint stirrings of rebellion within. A small voice, fragile but determined, saying, "Enough." Enough of living as though my heart is a burden. Enough of walking through life with measured steps, afraid of missteps that may never come. Enough of silencing the child who still dreams, who still believes, who still waits for me to set her free.

Perhaps one day, I will find her again. Perhaps one day, I will shatter the chains and let my soul breathe in the vastness of the sky. I will run without fear, laugh without restraint, and love without conditions. I will reclaim the wonder I have buried and learn to see the world not as a place of constraints but as a canvas for infinite possibility. And when that day comes, I will not mourn what was lost, for I will know that it was never truly gone. It was waiting, as patient as the stars, for me to look up and remember how to shine.

15. Chasing What Was Never Ours

Beneath the velvet canopy of the night,
Where stars blink softly, eternal and bright,
We stand as shadows, small and confined,
Our hearts consumed by a restless mind.

The moon hangs above, a silver ghost,
Silent witness to humanity's boast.
We long for its glow, its celestial grace,
Unseeing the light etched into our face.

The waves whisper secrets to the shores they kiss,
A reminder of all the beauty we miss.
Yet we gaze beyond, to horizons unknown,
Forsaking the treasures that are already our own.

The trees, their roots deep, their branches high,
Do not question the vastness of the sky.
But we, as humans, with hearts of clay,
Compare our own paths to others each day.

"Her stars burn brighter," we silently scream,
"His journey flows smoother, his waters gleam."
But the truth, elusive as the northern light,
Hides within us, concealed from sight.

The galaxies swirl in their cosmic dance,
Each star content in its own expanse.
Yet we, with our hunger, ache to compete,
Chasing a dream that keeps us incomplete.

The ocean, vast with its ceaseless tide,
Knows no envy, no need to deride.
Its depths hold mysteries, its surface shines,
Untroubled by whispers of better designs.

Still, we wander, unyielding in chase,
Seeking in others what we can't embrace.
The laughter of children, the warmth of a smile,
Forgotten as we measure worth by the mile.

Our hearts, like clocks, tick away the years,
Filling their chambers with doubts and fears.
Skin stretched thin from the weight we bear,
Eyes dulled by longing, gazing elsewhere.

The constellations above hold no feud,
No star feels lesser, no light subdued.
But here we stand, fragile and blind,
Chaining our souls with a comparing mind.

When will we pause, and truly see,
The beauty of just letting ourselves be?
The hand that we hold, the air we breathe,
The wonder beneath the lives we weave.

For the brightest moon can't calm the waves,
And the tallest tree won't silence caves.
Each has its purpose, its singular tone,
Why must we feel we are less alone?

Perhaps one day, when stars fade from sight,
And silence blankets the endless night,
We'll know the truth that the skies proclaim:
No two hearts are meant to burn the same.

Until then, the moon will continue to glow,
The tides will rise, the rivers will flow.
Nature whispers, with gentle care,
"To compare is human, but joy is rare."

So let us be still, with our heads held high,
And cease the longing for a brighter sky.
For the beauty we seek, the love we crave,
Is already ours—no need to enslave.

Ripples of reflection

The stars, eternal witnesses of human folly, watch silently as we stand beneath their shimmering gaze, yearning for a brilliance that mirrors their light. We, fragile creatures of boundless desire, tether ourselves to the illusion of more—more beauty, more success, more significance. Our hearts, crafted to feel joy in simplicity, instead become vessels for longing, overfilled with whispers of inadequacy and echoes of comparisons that sting like thorns. We stare at the moon, its face serene, and envy its unwavering glow, unaware that even it borrows its light, content to reflect rather than outshine. The rivers carve their paths with persistence, the trees stretch toward the heavens without questioning their worth, and the waves rise and fall in rhythm with the earth's heartbeat. Yet we, with all our wisdom and awareness, remain blind to the treasure of what we hold, constantly peering over the fence of our own lives to covet another's garden.

It is the human curse and gift—to feel deeply, to dream endlessly, but also to measure relentlessly. We break our spirits against the walls of imagined shortcomings, unable to see that the universe itself thrives in its differences. Every star does not seek to burn brighter than the next; every wave does not long to rise higher than the tide before it. But in our hearts, fragile and wild, lies a contradiction too heavy to carry yet impossible to put down—a craving for perfection in a world that was never meant to be perfect.

And so, we move through life like shadows chasing light, our skin bearing the scars of self-inflicted wounds, our eyes blind to the miracles that rest quietly in our palms. Perhaps the stars, in their infinite wisdom, mourn for us, wishing we could see what they have always known: that beauty is not in comparison, but in coexistence; not in longing for another's flame, but in tending to the fire within. Let this truth wash over us like the tides—unrelenting, cleansing, freeing. Let us learn from the moon to shine without needing to compete, from the rivers to flow without demanding recognition, and from the trees to grow simply because it is in their nature to reach for the sky.

16. In the Absence of Noise

In the quiet void where no voices stir,
Where silence sings like a distant purr,
I stand alone, not lost, but found,
In the emptiness that wraps me round.

The world outside, a storm in disguise,
Crashes with chaos, blind to my cries,
But here, in this space of sacred grace,
I meet my own heart, face to face.

How strange, how rare, this peaceful balm,
In a world so frenzied, where none stay calm.
The wind whispers secrets no ear can hear,
And in the stillness, I draw near.

The sea, it roars a song unknown,
A rhythm that speaks to the soul alone.
Its waves, they beckon with endless might,
Yet I stand still, bathed in moonlight.

The stars—each a story, each a soul,
Glitter above, making me whole.
They don't rush, they don't yearn,
They simply shine, while we burn.

A single tree stands, ancient and wise,
Rooted deep beneath the skies.
It does not compare, it does not fight,
It simply exists, a quiet delight.

And I, like the tree, stand in my place,
Not seeking a lover, not chasing a race.
I breathe the air, I drink the night,
For here in solitude, I find my light.

My heart, once torn by a thousand pleas,
Now beats in time with the whispering breeze.
Each pulse a reminder of the strength inside,
That blooms when there's no one to hide.

For in the quiet, there's no need for masks,
No roles to play, no questions to ask.
I am not who they think I should be,
But the person I've learned to set free.

The rivers may flow, the mountains may climb,
But I am not bound by the hands of time.
For in solitude, I am vast, I am whole,
A universe exists within my soul.

There's no rush to be something I'm not,
No need to chase what I've already sought.
In the stillness, I learn to understand,

That I am enough, just as I stand.

I do not need to fill the space,
For it is in emptiness that I find grace.
Like the moon, I am whole in my phases,
A quiet rhythm in life's endless mazes.

The world may weep, the stars may cry,
But in this solitude, I find the sky.
It's a gentle ache, a soft rebirth,
The soul returning to its worth.

No longer bound by others' eyes,
I see the truth that lies inside.
The beauty of solitude is not in its quiet,
But in the peace that comes when we riot.

Against the noise, against the plea,
To fit in, to belong, to simply be.
For in the absence of all things, I find,
The wild, untamed truth of my own mind.

And here, I rest—beneath the skies,
In solitude, where freedom lies.
For in this sacred, silent grace,
I find myself, I find my place.

Ripples of reflection

In the stillness of solitude, the world pauses, and the heart finds itself adrift in an ocean of its own making. It is here, in the profound silence, that we confront the deepest parts of ourselves—the places we keep hidden, even from the mirror. The world rushes on with its demands, its ceaseless noise, its voices telling us what to do, how to be, and who to become. But in solitude, there is no expectation. There are no rules. It is just you and the expanse of everything that you are—every fear, every joy, every sorrow that has been swept under the rug of daily life. It is a confrontation so raw that it feels as though the very sky above might crack open, revealing the weight of every unspoken word and every shattered dream. In these moments, when the heart beats in isolation, there is no distraction to dull the ache, no escape from the deep well of longing that sits within. Yet, strangely, it is in this very ache that we find our most honest selves. The beauty of solitude lies not in its emptiness, but in the fullness it brings—the space to hear your own thoughts, to feel your own breath, to reclaim pieces of yourself lost in the chaos of life. We are constantly surrounded by voices, expectations, and the pressure to belong, to conform, to move with the flow. But solitude strips all of that away, leaving behind a person, naked and raw, standing in the vastness of their own truth. It is here, alone with your own thoughts, that the greatest transformation takes place. You will confront the storms that rage within, the fears you have buried deep, and the desires you thought you had forgotten. And in that confrontation, there is a quiet surrender, a realization that perhaps it is only in the stillness, in the aloneness, that we can truly understand who we are. The solitude will whisper its secrets—the ones the world around us never had the time to speak—and in that silence, we might find our deepest answers, our truest selves. We may be alone, but in that solitude, we are finally free.

17. Unheard, Yet Felt

Beneath the quiet heavens where silence lies,
There are words we hold, like unspoken cries.
Heavy as stones that we bury deep,
Hidden away where shadows sleep.

We carry them, though they never escape,
Silent confessions our hearts can't reshape.
Each one a weight, too fierce to bear,
A burden of sorrow, of things left in prayer.

The spaces between us, they twist and they ache,
A void in the silence, for heaven's sake.
How often we stand, face to face,
But never release the truths we chase.

In moments we could, we choose not to speak,
Fear choking the voice that's timid and weak.
And so they remain, these words unsaid,
Lodged in our throats, heavy as lead.

We carry them like a haunting refrain,
Silent echoes of joy, love, and pain.
The things we should've, could've, dared to declare,
The warmth that was hidden, the love left in air.

But they sit in our chests, suffocating our grace,
Filling the spaces we cannot erase.
For words left unspoken are not just a strain,
They're like ghosts that return to haunt us again.

Oh, how we yearn to speak our hearts free,
But the silence constricts, as vast as the sea.
We wish we could shout, wish we could cry,
But fear holds us captive, and time slips by.

We remain in our prisons, with walls made of fear,
Unable to voice the things we hold dear.
The silence becomes a cage we cannot escape,
The words we long for, forever on tape.

And the weight of them grows, grows with each day,
As moments pass by, as time slips away.
For the longer we stay silent, the harder it gets,
Until we are buried in our own regrets.

The things we didn't say, the things we concealed,
They fester and swell, our wounds never healed.
We walk through life carrying this load,
Each step a reminder of the road we have slowed.

In the still of the night, in the quiet of the dawn,
We wonder what might have been, what's gone.
If we'd only spoken, if we'd only been bold,

The heartache, the regret, might not have taken hold.

But the words remain locked, as cold as the stone,
And we suffer alone with the things we've never known.
The weight of unspoken words presses us deep,
An endless sorrow, an eternal sweep.

The echoes of silence call louder with time,
As moments slip by, as we climb and we climb.
We wonder if we'll ever set them free,
If the silence will always remain in our plea.

But perhaps, just perhaps, one day we'll find,
The courage to speak, to heal, to unwind.
Until that day, we are left with the weight,
The things we couldn't say, the silence we hate.

For the weight of unspoken words is a heavy toll,
It buries the soul, it tears at the whole.
But one day, when silence has had its say,
We'll release the words that were meant for today.

And when they are freed, the heart will unbind,
The weight of the unsaid no longer confined.
Until that day, we will carry the strain,
Of all that was left, and all that remains.

Ripples of reflection

In the spaces between breaths, where words dare not tread, a weight settles like a storm cloud, heavy with unspoken truths. The silence, though invisible to the eye, presses down with the force of mountains, squeezing the air from our lungs, leaving only the echo of what we should have said. How often we find ourselves standing at the edge of a conversation, afraid to speak, afraid to release the words we know are meant to heal, yet are too afraid to voice. They sit in the chest, heavy, like stones dropped into the depths of an ocean, sinking deeper and deeper into the abyss of what we refuse to acknowledge. Each unspoken word, each paused sentence, is a fracture in the very foundation of our being. It builds within us, unseen yet unrelenting, as we carry the weight of thoughts and emotions that could never find the light of day. And so, we silence ourselves, thinking that perhaps it's better this way, that the quiet will protect us from the vulnerability that words might expose. But all we do is create a prison for our hearts, walls too high to scale, locks too firm to break.

We convince ourselves that the things left unsaid are harmless, mere whispers in the wind that will eventually be forgotten, but they are not. They are thorns buried deep beneath the skin, festering in the quietest corners of our souls. Each day they grow, twisting and tightening, until they become a knot in our chest that no amount of time can unravel. The silence becomes deafening, the weight of unspoken words a constant companion, one we cannot shake, no matter how far we run. It is there, always present, like the shadow of a past we cannot escape. And in the quiet, we feel the longing, the ache, for the release of those words, for the opportunity to let go of the burden that has come to define us. But we are trapped, not by others, but by ourselves, by our own fear of what those words might bring. We wonder if, when spoken, they will bring relief or more pain, if the truth will heal us or leave us even more broken than we already are.

Yet, in our silence, the world continues to spin. The sun rises, the moon shifts through its phases, the stars burn bright above us, indifferent to the weight we carry. The oceans swell, the wind moves through the trees, life moves on as we remain still, caught in the grip of all that we have failed to say. And still, we hope. We hope that one day, the silence will break. We hope that, at some point, the words we have buried so deep will be freed, to float like dandelion seeds in the air, carried away by the winds of release. But until that day comes, we endure the quiet, the hollow space between us and those we love, between our hearts and the world around us. We endure the aching silence, the reminder that sometimes, the things we fail to speak are the things that weigh on us most. And as we wait, we wonder if we will ever find the courage to speak the words that could set us free, or if, perhaps, we have already waited too long.

18. The Mirage of Power

We build our walls, strong and high,
Hiding from the world, beneath a sky.
We grasp the reins with hands so frail,
Fighting against the winds that wail.

In the stillness of a desperate night,
We beg for solace, a flicker of light.
But the stars remain distant, cold, and far,
A cruel reminder of our broken star.

We chart our course with all our might,
But the tides, they twist, they break our sight.
The ocean's roar calls, demanding control,
Yet we, so small, play our fragile role.

We rise each day, consumed by pride,
Convinced that we alone can guide the tide.
But the winds, they whisper in our ears,
Telling tales of ancient fears.

We try to tame the storm's fierce eye,
To bend the sky, to make it comply.
Yet the heavens laugh, a mocking sound,
For we're just dancers, caught and bound.

The winds may scream, the heavens cry,
And we cling to hope, but we don't know why.
For each second lost, we grasp at air,
Falling further with each despair.

We shape the world, thinking we are wise,
But it spins away, beyond our eyes.
Each twist of fate, each cruel surprise,
Shakes us to the core, as truth defies.

We bind ourselves with chains of pride,
But the stars above, they never hide.
The more we grasp, the less we see,
We are not the masters; we are the plea.

We clutch and clutch, but we fall apart,
Lost in the illusion of a broken heart.
For no matter how much we try to bind,
The universe mocks the way we mind.

The rivers run, the mountains stand,
We try to break them with trembling hands.
But the earth hums a melody we can't understand,
And in that song, we'll never command.

The harder we fight, the deeper we fall,
A desperate scream, a hollow call.
The wind laughs at our feeble quest,

For in the chaos, we are not blessed.

We think we hold the answers tight,
But the world reminds us, year by year,
That in the grand dance of endless time,
We are but whispers in the divine.

The mountains rise, the oceans roar,
And we, so lost, continue to implore.
For every step, every tear we shed,
Leads us to places where fear is fed.

The more we fight, the more we break,
Chasing control we cannot make.
We clutch at life, desperate, blind,
But we are lost, untethered, confined.

In the end, when all is said,
We're scattered like ashes, left for dead.
For control is an illusion we build in vain,
A dream that never sees the light of day.

The illusion of control, fleeting and true,
A lie we cling to, a view askew.
But in the universe's grand design,
We are but stars, lost in time.

We release, we let go, we break free,
And in the letting, we cease to be.

For in surrender, we find our soul,
Not by controlling, but letting go of the goal.

In the storm, we lose our grace,
In chaos, we find our place.
And though we're small, adrift in the night,
In surrender, we discover the light.

The illusion, though real, fades in the wind,
As the earth spins on, unpinned.
And in the end, we find our peace,
In the letting go, our hearts released.

For we are not in charge, not in command,
We are the dust, the grain of sand.
The earth moves on, the stars still sing,
And we, in surrender, are everything.

Ripples of reflection

In the vast, unyielding silence of the universe, we stand, trembling and small, grasping desperately at the fleeting moments that slip through our fingers like grains of sand. We build our walls, high and unshakable, convinced they will protect us from the chaos that rages outside, from the winds that howl in the distance. With every breath, we tighten our grip on life, believing that if we just hold on long enough, we can command the world to bend to our will. But the more we clutch, the more the earth slips through our hands, the more we realize that the universe does not bend, does not yield to our pleas.

Each moment, we build our castles in the sky, trying to shape the stars, the ocean, the mountains, believing that by controlling them, we can conquer the unknown. Yet, with every step we take, we are met by the fierce tides of fate, the winds of change, pushing us further from our illusions of power. We fight, we struggle, and with each struggle, we lose ourselves a little more, unraveling like threads pulled by the relentless forces of the cosmos. Our walls crumble, our grip loosens, but we still hold on, stubborn in our belief that if we just try harder, if we just hold tighter, we can somehow make everything fall into place.

But the truth, as cold and unyielding as the stars above us, is that control is an illusion. The world moves with a rhythm we cannot comprehend, a pulse that beats beyond our reach. The earth spins, the tides roll in, the winds blow with a fury we cannot tame. And in our desperate attempts to control it all, we find only loss, only the gnawing emptiness of being caught in a dance we were never meant to lead. The more we fight, the more we are consumed by the very thing we sought to master.

Yet, in the quiet moments, when the world falls away, we are left with a whisper — a quiet call to surrender. To stop struggling, to stop holding on, and to simply let go. It is in this release that we discover the secret we have longed for: that we are not meant to control the universe. We are meant to move with it, to follow its rhythms, to become part of the dance that unfolds before us. And in that surrender, we find the peace we have been searching for, the peace that was always there, waiting for us to stop trying to hold it all together.

For in the act of letting go, we find our strength. In the absence of control, we discover the freedom to simply be. The universe does not need our commands; it moves with a grace we could never understand, and in that grace, we find our place. The tides will rise, the winds will howl, the stars will burn bright — and we, small as we are, will simply be, caught in the beauty of the dance, no longer needing to lead, no longer needing to control. Just moving, just breathing, just being. And in that stillness, in that surrender, we are free.

19. Through the Veil of Hours

Beneath the stars, so distant, bright,
We chase the hours, lost to the night.
Each second slips like sand in streams,
Too swift to catch, too far from dreams.

We stand beneath its crushing weight,
The hands of time that never wait.
No pause, no breath, no gentle sway,
Only the echo of yesterday.

The sun ascends, then dips again,
Each rise, each fall, a silent pain.
We stretch our hands, we stretch our hearts,
But time, uncaring, tears apart.

In twilight's glow, we search for truth,
Through moments lost and days of youth.
But time, relentless in its flow,
Leaves us grasping what we'll never know.

Each face we love, each word we speak,
Slips through the cracks, the ones we seek.

THROUGH THE EYES OF SEVENTEEN

No hand can halt this endless race,
We find ourselves just out of place.

The whispers of the past grow faint,
Lost in the wind, untouched by saint.
We try to hold them, cherish tight,
But time erases day and night.

The memories that once burned bright,
Now fade away in endless flight.
Like shadows cast on walls so tall,
We cannot hold them, though we call.

We cling to moments, held in dreams,
But time is ruthless, or so it seems.
It takes and takes, it swallows whole,
Until we're empty, heart and soul.

Oh, how we wish to freeze the tide,
To stop the world, to turn and hide.
But time's a river, swift and strong,
Its flow relentless, right or wrong.

We try to catch it, hold it near,
To slow the moments that we fear.
But like the wind, it slips our grasp,
A cruel illusion we can't clasp.

We chase the hours, we run the race,
We try to win, but fall from grace.
Each step we take, each breath we make,
Is one more memory we forsake.

The seconds slip, the minutes fall,
The hours stretch and yet stand tall.
And still we chase, though time has wings,
We never learn the worth of things.

And when the years have come and gone,
When we've long faded, passed and drawn,
We'll see the lessons time has taught,
The battles lost, the battles fought.

For time will break us, bend our will,
It winds and winds, a force to kill.
Yet still we stand, we still we fight,
We strive to hold what's out of sight.

The endless rush, the endless race,
We never stop to find our place.
But in the end, we see the truth,
That time's not ours, it never soothes.

In time's great tide, we lose the fight,
We search for dawn, we search for night.
But in its arms, we cannot flee,
For time belongs to none but free.

So still we walk through nights and days,
In time's embrace, in endless haze.
We march forward, though we are torn,
Through every dusk, through every dawn.

For in this march, we find our way,
We lose the race, but still we stay.
The echoes of what once was clear,
Now distant, fading year by year.

And when the final moments come,
When time has left, we are undone.
We'll see that in the end, we find,
It's not the race, but peace of mind.

The time we spent, the time we lost,
In chasing what's beyond the cost.
Yet still, we march, we still we fight,
Until we find our quiet light.

Ripples of reflection

Time—the one force we cannot defy, the endless river in which we are mere particles, tumbling helplessly, never to be whole again. It rushes forward with no regard for our cries, our desires, our hearts that seek to hold onto something, anything that will anchor us in a world that seems to slip away the moment we grasp it. We try to build our castles of certainty, to cement our feet into the earth, but with every tick of the clock, the sand beneath us shifts, the ground trembles, and the sky—so vast and indifferent—does not wait for us to catch up. We wish for a moment of stillness, a single breath where the world pauses, just long enough for us to recognize the beauty in what we have, the joy in the present, the treasures of our fleeting days. Yet, as we stretch to catch the moments as they flee, we find ourselves chasing after shadows, as time, with its cold hands, continues to unravel the very fabric of our existence. The faces we love blur into the past; the words we left unsaid echo like whispers lost in the wind. We are left with the cruel understanding that time does not belong to us—it owns us. But within this truth, buried deep within the relentless tide, is the secret we so often miss—the beauty is not in holding on, but in learning to let go, to embrace the rush of it all, to dance with time as it sweeps us along. For in every moment of struggle, in every tear we shed for what we can't keep, we find something pure: the undeniable, irreplaceable miracle of being alive in the first place. To be alive, to be swept by time, is not a tragedy, but the gift of knowing that we have truly lived, however briefly, however imperfectly. And so, in the midst of time's storm, we find our peace—not in stopping it, but in surrendering to the flow, in trusting that in the end, it was never about the minutes we missed, but the moments we chose to live within.

20. Seasons of the soul

Beneath the shivering breath of the autumn wind,
I watched you fade, like leaves unpinned.
Once vibrant, you were a flame that burned so bright,
But now you're the dusk that follows day's light.

The sea, it whispers secrets of shifting tides,
And I, like a ship, lost where the storm resides.
You once held my hand, warm as spring's embrace,
Now, you're a shadow I can never trace.

In the spring, your eyes were the dawn's first rays,
A warmth that melted all of my gray days.
But with the turning earth, you turned away,
Like flowers that bloom just to decay.

I remember when we danced, without fear,
With hearts that beat in sync, crystal clear.
But seasons change, as all things do,
And I found myself looking at a stranger, too.

Your laughter once echoed in the summer breeze,
It was the peace in the thunder, the calm in the seas.
But now, that laughter fades into the night,
A distant sound, lost in twilight.

Like the summer sun that's swallowed by the dusk,
I find your presence now wrapped in a husk.
The waves, they crash with a sorrowful cry,
As you turn away, without a reason why.

Autumn falls, heavy with the weight of goodbye,
I watched you change beneath the bruised sky.
You, once the sun that filled my skies,
Now just a shadow, wearing a disguise.

The winds carry your voice, now distant, cold,
A love once tender, now turning bold.
What happened to the warmth we used to share?
Now it's a winter, too frozen to care.

Time, like the river, doesn't ask why,
It flows, and with it, we say goodbye.
You've become the storm, relentless, wild,
And I, the shore, forever beguiled.

The trees, they shed their leaves in the fall,
A symbol of how we both stand so small.
You walk away, and I stand here, bare,
With the wind carrying my silent prayer.

The ocean roars with the pain we deny,
As my heart breaks beneath a changeless sky.
Once, your smile was the calm after rain,

Now it's the thunder that strikes in vain.

Where did you go, in the silence of change?
Why does love become so estranged?
Like waves that crash, only to recede,
You left me with nothing but a heart that bleeds.

And yet, in the stillness of winter's reign,
I wait for you, to come back again.
For even the coldest storms must fade,
And even the most broken hearts must be remade.

But the winds, they whisper of truths untold,
Of stories of us that will never grow old.
The seasons are harsh, and love is cruel,
But life has a way of making us whole.

The moon may rise and the stars may fall,
But time will heal what's shattered, after all.
For in every winter, there's a spring yet to come,
And from the ashes, we can still become.

The ocean, vast and ever-moving, knows no end,
Just like the love I thought I could not mend.
For though the tides may ebb and flow,
They always find their way back to the shore below.

So, I wait. Wait for the dawn after the night,
For the first bloom of spring, pure and bright.

In the changing of seasons, I'll learn to see,
That some loves fade, but they set us free.

For in every tear shed, every loss we bear,
There's a lesson waiting, a soul laid bare.
And like the seasons, we too must change,
To find the peace in the winds that rearrange.

One day, I'll look to the horizon wide,
And know that I've loved, and been loved inside.
For seasons are fleeting, but hearts endure,
And in the end, we all find a way to be pure.

Ripples of reflection

As the ink fades from these pages, the heart beats in quiet anticipation, knowing that the end of one journey only marks the beginning of another. This collection of words, this mosaic of emotions, has been a fragile offering—a map of the soul's trials and triumphs, of the moments when we stood tall and the times we stumbled in the dark. Each poem, each whisper of thought, has been an echo of life as it truly is: fleeting, fragile, and yet, impossibly vast. The seasons of our hearts, like those of the earth, change with unrelenting speed. What we are now is not who we were, and who we will be is a mystery still unfolding. In this tapestry of shifting moments, there are truths we can no longer deny, truths that speak louder than any words we could ever write.

The journey we've taken is one of constant motion, like the tide that never ceases to rise and fall. With each verse, we've watched as the very landscape of our emotions has transformed before our eyes—like the ocean that kisses the shore with a tenderness that can only come after a storm, and the mountains that stand tall, not despite the winds, but because of them. We are all shaped by time, carved into who we are by the forces we cannot control, by the moments that slip through our fingers, by the seasons that do not wait. And yet, within this tide of change, we are always searching for something: a glimpse of ourselves we can hold onto, a moment of stillness amidst the storm, a whisper of understanding in a world that is constantly shifting beneath our feet.

And here, at the crossroads of this book's closing, we must ask ourselves: Are we not like the trees that bend in the wind, the stars that burn in the night sky, the waves that crash tirelessly against the shore? Are we not reflections of the very earth we inhabit—forever growing, forever changing, forever seeking to understand our place in the vast expanse of time? It is in this paradox that we exist, bound by the earth but reaching for the heavens, tethered to the past yet always moving toward the future.

As you read the final words, remember that there is beauty in the change, in the ebb and flow of our existence. The person you were yesterday is not the person you are today, and who you will be tomorrow is yet to be revealed. Like the ocean that whispers its secrets to the shore, like the trees that shed their leaves to bloom once more, so too do we evolve. And as this final verse is written, I ask you to let go of what you think you know, to embrace the unknown, and to find peace in the quiet chaos that surrounds us all.

For in the end, the truth is simple: We are the seasons. We are the stars. We are the earth beneath our feet and the heavens above our heads. And though we may change, though we may bend beneath the weight of it all, we will never truly break. We will rise again, with the same fire that once burned in our hearts, and we will carry on, knowing that this journey is one we make not alone, but together, as part of something far greater than ourselves.

Acknowledgements

This book, though bound in pages and ink, represents so much more than just written words. It is the product of years of effort, growth, love, and a network of people whose unwavering support has been the true foundation of everything I have created. With each poem, I reflect not only on my own experiences, but on the many hands that have guided me, inspired me, and stood by me as I crafted this collection. I am forever grateful to every single person who has touched my life, and I am humbled to be able to share this piece of myself with the world.

First and foremost, to my parents: there are no words grand enough to express my love and gratitude to you both. From the very beginning, you have been my foundation—my rock and my compass. Your unconditional love has been the guiding light in my life, and it is because of you that I have the strength to chase my dreams. You believed in me even when I couldn't believe in myself, and your quiet encouragement has always been the wind beneath my wings. Through every trial, every tear, and every joy, you have been there. Your sacrifices, your endless patience, your constant care—these are the things that have shaped me into who I am today. You've never once questioned my path, but rather, you have supported me with your boundless faith in my abilities. It is because of you that I am able to stand here today, proud of what I have created. This book, my words, and every dream I pursue are dedicated to you both, the most extraordinary people I will ever know. I hope I can live up to the example you've set for me, one of strength, resilience, and unwavering love.

ACKNOWLEDGEMENTS

To my friends—where do I even begin? You have been my constant companions, my partners in crime, and my biggest supporters. You have celebrated my victories, offered a shoulder during my defeats, and always reminded me of my worth even when I couldn't see it myself. Each one of you has touched my life in a unique and irreplaceable way. Whether we have shared years of memories or moments that lasted but a brief instant, your presence in my life has been immeasurable. You've laughed with me, cried with me, and stood by my side as I've ventured through every twist and turn of this journey. The bond we share goes beyond just friendship—it is a bond built on trust, shared experiences, and the kind of connection that transcends time and distance.

I want to thank those of you who have believed in my writing, even when it felt like a distant dream. Your encouragement has been a guiding force, pushing me to believe in myself when the self-doubt was overwhelming. To my friends who have read early drafts of my poems and offered their honest feedback, thank you for your unwavering honesty and support. Your feedback was crucial, and your belief in me gave me the courage to take this book to completion. I am incredibly fortunate to have such an amazing group of people around me who have cheered me on from the sidelines, pushing me to reach further and dream bigger. Without you, I truly would not be here.

To those who have walked with me through the darker chapters of life, your presence has been a healing balm. Sometimes, it takes the stormiest of days to find clarity, and in those days, you helped me to see the light that still existed, even in the shadows. Your kindness and your empathy gave me the strength to continue, to write, to pour my heart out into these pages. Life is never easy, and sometimes the path feels lonely, but you reminded me that I was never truly alone. Whether you've been a part of my life for years or whether we've only recently crossed paths, your support has made all the difference. Thank you for being my refuge when the world felt heavy, for being my safe place to rest and regroup, and for helping me to rediscover my passion for life and for writing.

To the mentors and teachers who have guided me, challenged me, and nurtured my creativity, I am endlessly grateful. You have shaped me not only as a writer but as a person, and the lessons I've learned from you extend far beyond the classroom. Your wisdom has been invaluable, and your belief in my potential has driven me to reach for greater heights. The encouragement and guidance you've provided have given me the confidence to pursue my passion for writing and to take it seriously as a craft. You've taught me that writing is not just about putting words on paper, but about pouring your soul into the work, and for that, I will always be thankful.

To those who have believed in the power of words—those who have read my work, shared their thoughts, and inspired me to keep going, thank you. The written word has always been a source of solace for me, a way to express my deepest thoughts and emotions. Knowing that my words have reached others, have touched hearts, and have sparked conversations, is a gift beyond measure. This book is as much yours as it is mine. Without the support of readers, of fellow writers, and of all those who champion the arts, this dream would have remained unrealized. Thank you for giving my words a place in this world, for embracing the rawness of emotion, and for reminding me of the power that art has to connect us all.

To the ones who have left my life, yet shaped me in ways I cannot fully explain—thank you for the lessons, however difficult they may have been.

You taught me the value of resilience, the importance of self-love, and the need for growth. Sometimes, the people who leave us make the most lasting impact, and while our paths may no longer cross, your influence remains in my work, in my heart, and in the way I approach life. I carry your lessons with me, woven into the fabric of who I am today.

Finally, to the universe, for guiding me on this journey. For the moments of inspiration, for the quiet whispers of creativity, and for the opportunity to turn my passion into something tangible. Writing this book has been a journey of discovery, and it is one that I will cherish forever. I have learned more about myself, about the world around me, and about the power of art and expression than I ever imagined I would.

To anyone who has ever touched my life in any way—thank you. Every interaction, every conversation, every shared experience has shaped the person I am and contributed to the creation of this book. It is impossible to list every individual who has impacted me, but know that each of you is forever etched into the pages of my heart.

This book is a culmination of not just my efforts, but the love and support of so many. It stands as a testament to the power of connection, to the strength of community, and to the belief that no one is ever truly alone. With every page turned, I honor those who have walked with me, who have lifted me, and who have believed in me. I hope that these poems serve as a reflection of the gratitude I carry, and that they inspire others as much as the people in my life have inspired me.

Thank you, from the depths of my heart.

About The Author

At 17, I find myself standing at the precipice of both the past and the future, looking back at the path I've traveled and forward to the unknown terrain I have yet to explore. Writing has always been my outlet, a way to capture the moments, thoughts, and feelings that swirl in my mind, giving them form and expression. It's my way of understanding the world, of making sense of the chaos that often surrounds me, and it's through these words that I've learned to breathe a little easier.

The world around me, shaped by the heavy expectations of society, has often felt stifling. From the moment I could understand the concept of rules, norms, and "appropriate" behavior, I felt the weight of these invisible chains pulling me in directions I didn't want to go. These constraints, these things that were supposed to keep me in line, to make me "fit" into the mold society had created, always felt wrong. I've spent my entire life trying to break free from them, only to be reminded time and time again that the world doesn't look kindly on those who stray too far from the norm. But in these pages, in the collection of poems you hold in your hands, I've found my freedom.

Through writing, I've been able to confront these feelings head-on. I wanted to express the thoughts and emotions I've carried with me throughout my teenage years—the confusion, the frustration, the longing, the joy, and the sorrow—all of it. Every poem is a piece of me, an honest reflection of the complex tapestry of my life up until this point. It is my way of giving my thoughts the validation they've always craved, of showing myself that my feelings are real and that they matter.

I've often wondered why we, as a society, put so much emphasis on conforming, on fitting in, and on following paths that others have already paved for us. In a world where everyone is constantly being told what to do, how to behave, and how to think, it's easy to feel like you're suffocating. I felt that suffocation deeply. I couldn't breathe in a world that demanded I be something I wasn't, something I could never be. There were times when I thought that perhaps I was the problem, that maybe I was just too sensitive or too rebellious. But the truth is, the problem wasn't me; it was the world around me. A world that insisted on categorizing and labeling everything, a world that didn't allow for individuality, for free thought, for the beautiful mess of human emotions.

But I refused to be broken by it. I refused to let society dictate my path, to tell me that my voice didn't matter. So, I wrote. I wrote about everything I felt. I wrote about the parts of me that I kept hidden from the world, the parts I was too scared to share, and the parts I longed to shout to the heavens. Writing became my rebellion, my form of protest, my way of refusing to be swallowed by a world that was too busy trying to make everyone the same.

These poems are my truth. They are the echoes of my soul, the words I could never speak aloud, the feelings I could never show to anyone. They represent my attempts to understand who I am, to find meaning in the chaos, and to make sense of the contradictions within me. Through each poem, I've discovered something new about myself—about my desires, my fears, my hopes, and my dreams. This book is not just a collection of words; it is my heart on paper, laid bare for the world to see.

In writing this book, I've come to understand that the rules and expectations that society places on us are not meant to define who we are; they are just obstacles meant to test our resilience. Every moment of confusion, every moment of doubt, and every moment of pain has only made me stronger. It has made me more determined to hold on to my truth, to never let the world silence my voice, no matter how loud it gets. I've learned that it is okay to question, to feel, to be imperfect, and to break free from the mold. In fact, it is more than okay—it is necessary.

This book is my gift to anyone who has ever felt suffocated by society's demands. It is for anyone who has ever wanted to scream out their thoughts, their feelings, and their truth but was too afraid to do so. It is for the ones who don't fit in, for the ones who feel lost, for the ones who question everything. It is a reminder that we don't have to follow the crowd, that we don't have to live by other people's rules. We are allowed to create our own path, to follow our own heart, and to live in our own truth.

As I continue my journey through life, I hope to keep writing, to keep sharing my experiences, and to keep pushing back against the world that would have me shrink. I am learning, slowly but surely, that I am enough as I am. And that is the message I hope you take from this book—that you are enough too, just as you are, with all your flaws, all your imperfections, and all your dreams.

This book is for anyone who has ever felt misunderstood, for anyone who has ever wondered if they were alone in their struggles. You are not alone. We are all here, sharing this space, struggling, growing, and finding our way. Through the power of words, we can break free, validate our feelings, and reclaim our voices. And that is something worth fighting for.

Signing off,
Sargam Singh.

www.ingramcontent.com/pod-product-compliance
Lightning Source LLC
Chambersburg PA
CBHW031150130726

47988CB00006B/2610